Holiday Inspirations
Arranged by Paul Johnston

AF207509

Music is a huge part of what makes Christmas so special. This collection contains some of my favorite music of the season. With these familiar pieces, I strived to bring something fresh and new to each selection by using jazz reharmonizations and different styles. Each arrangement contains a written-out solo section, so you can sound like you're improvising even if you're not a jazz musician. I encourage you to experiment with your own improvisations as well. I hope you enjoy playing these arrangements and sharing the music with family and friends at home, in recitals, or in church. Merry Christmas!

—Paul Johnston

Alfred

Alfred Music
P.O. Box 10003
Van Nuys, CA 91410-0003
alfred.com

ISBN-10: 0-7390-8289-2
ISBN-13: 978-0-7390-8289-8

Angels We Have Heard on High

Traditional
Arr. Paul Johnston

pedal as needed

Away in a Manger

James R. Murray
Arr. Paul Johnston

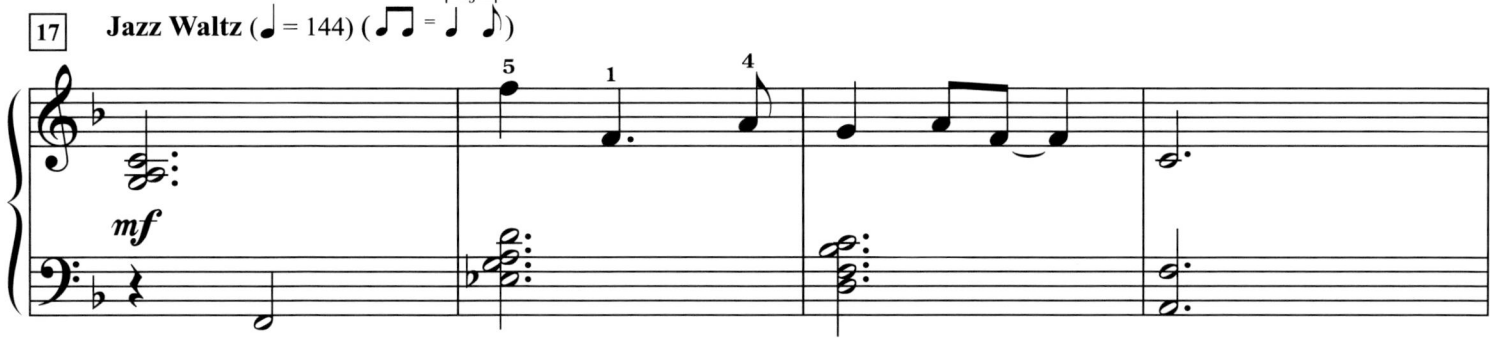

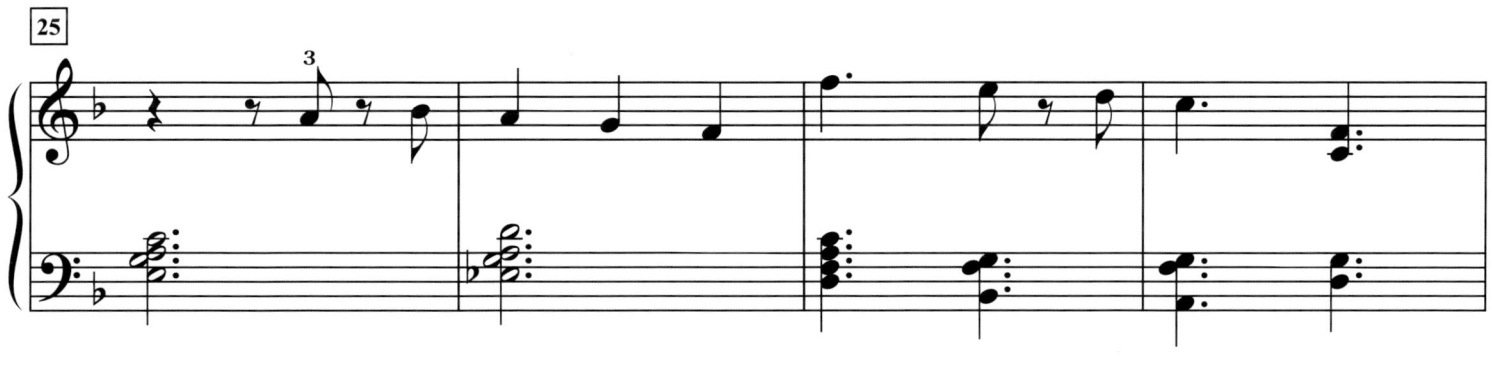

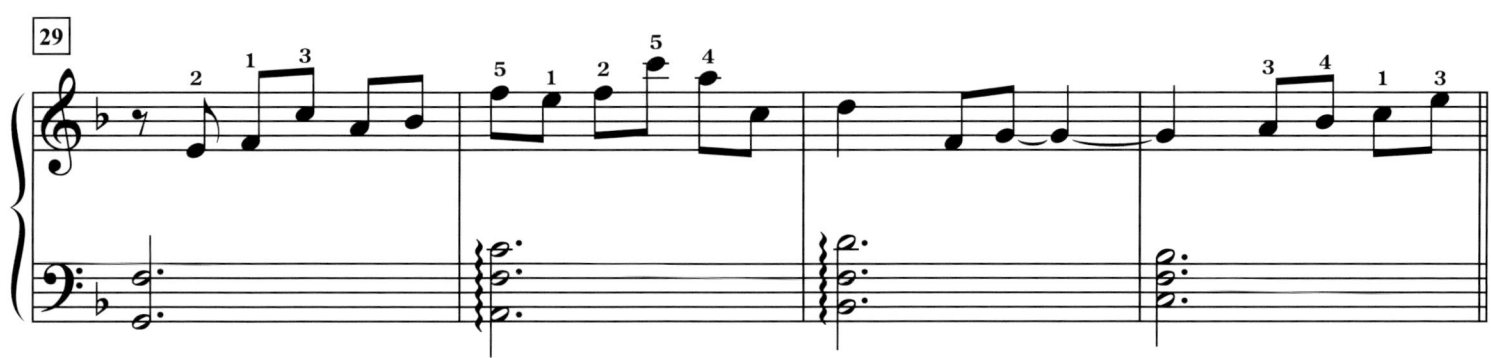

(melody)

Bring a Torch, Jeannette, Isabella

Traditional French Carol
Arr. Paul Johnston

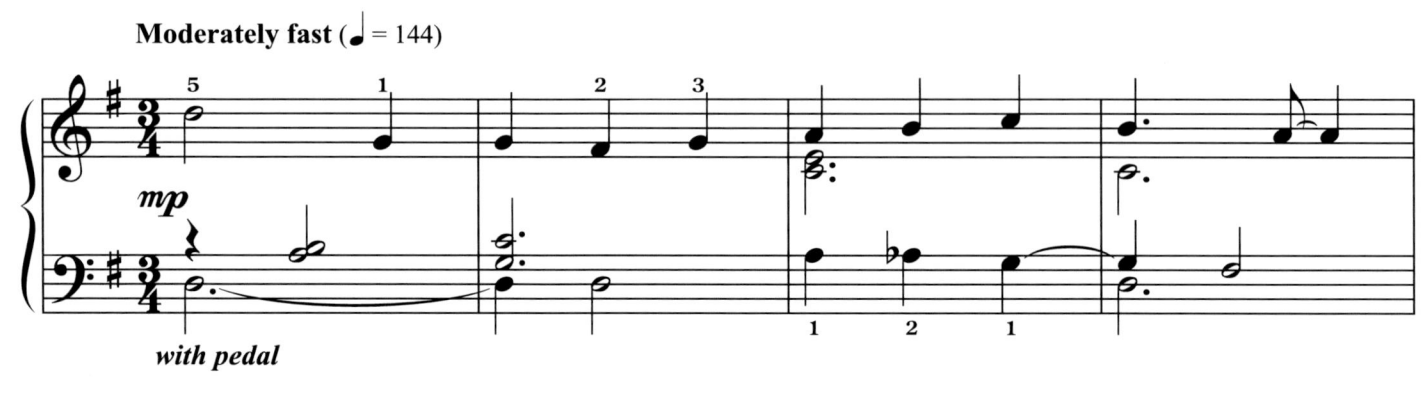

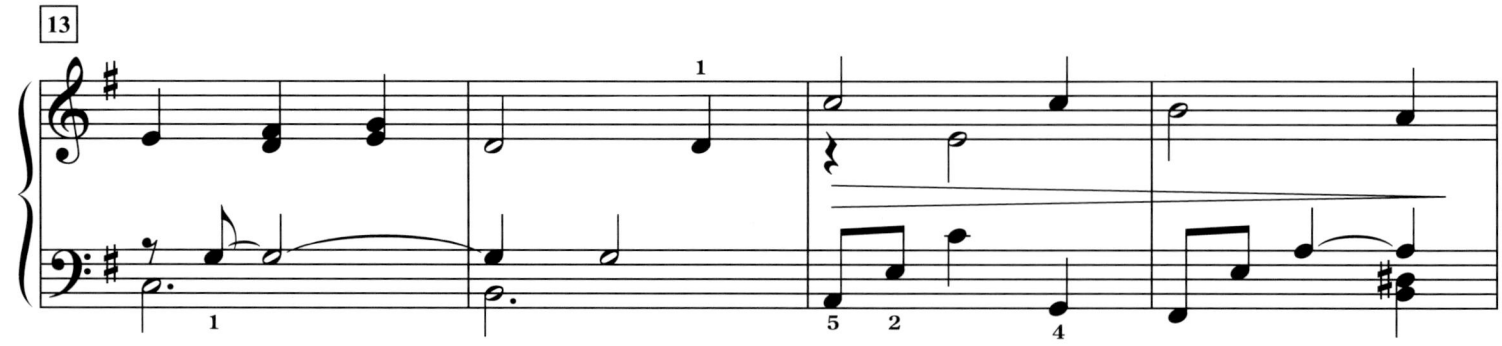

DECK THE HALLS

Traditional
Arr. Paul Johnston

God Rest Ye Merry, Gentlemen

Traditional
Arr. Paul Johnston

It Came Upon the Midnight Clear

Richard S. Willis
Arr. Paul Johnston

Jingle Bells

James Pierpoint
Arr. Paul Johnston

Joy to the World

George Frideric Handel
Arr. Paul Johnston

Lo! How a Rose E'er Blooming

Michael Praetorius
Arr. Paul Johnston

Silent Night

Franz Grüber
Arr. Paul Johnston